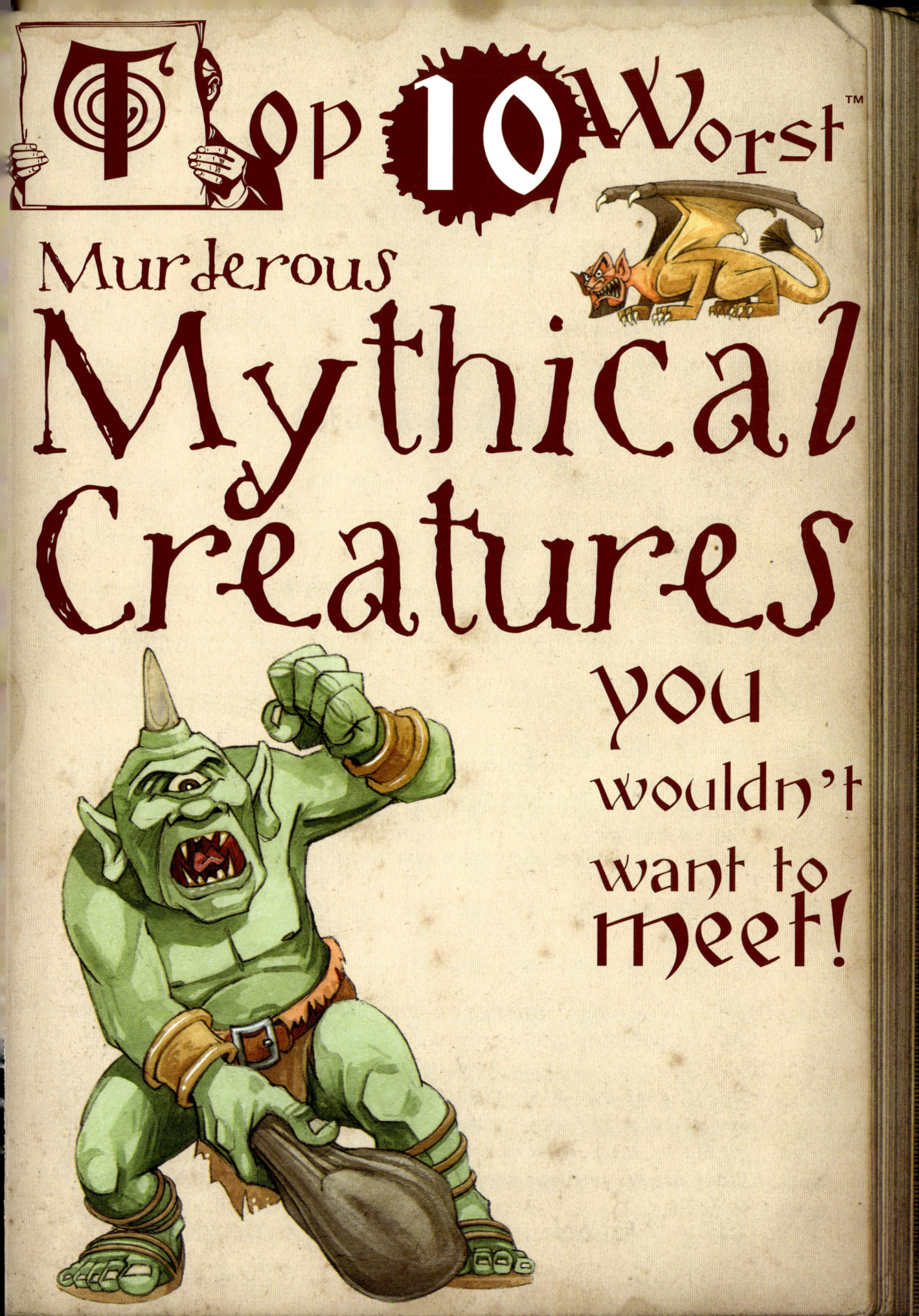

Top 10 Worst™

Murderous Mythical Creatures

you wouldn't want to meet!

An Imprint of Sterling Publishing
387 Park Avenue South
New York, NY 10016

Series creator: David Salariya
Author: Fiona Macdonald
Editor: Jamie Pitman
Illustrations: David Antram

ISBN 978-1-4351-5038-6 (HB)

Manufactured in Heshan, Guangdong Province, China
Lot #:
2 4 6 8 10 9 7 5 3 1
06/13

Top 10 Worst™

Murderous Mythical Creatures

you wouldn't want to meet!

Grrrrr!

Created & designed by
David Salariya

Illustrated by
David Antram

Written by
Fiona Macdonald

Sandy Creek
NEW YORK

Contents

Mythical mysteries!

Myths are stories with meanings. They can be true and false, funny and serious, and frightening and comforting all at the same time. In myths you will meet gods and heroes, villains and victims, the brave and the beautiful—together with the strange, the silly, and the very, very scary.

I always wanted to be famous!

fantastic and fabulous

Myths feature many fantastic and fabulous animals. These mythical creatures are magical, mysterious, marvelous—but beware! They are not always friendly… Ammut? She'll gobble you up! Grendel? He'll tear you limb from limb! The troll? He'll crunch your bones! The shining winged serpent brings death; horrid Baba Yaga chases children. Even the ancient Greek centaurs (part human, part horse) have a nasty side to them!

Voices from the past

Most myths are thousands of years old. They record ancient history and preserve old customs and beliefs. Until around 1800, many myths were never written down. Instead, they were memorized by generations of storytellers and passed on by word of mouth.

Shudder!

Ooooh!

Eeek!

Shiver!

Tremble!

6

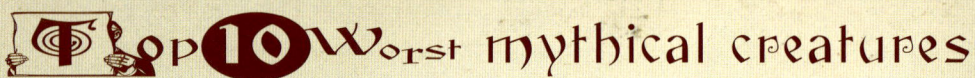

A world of wonders

Weird and wonderful creatures are found in myths from all around the world.

Thunderbird
(North America)

Kraken
(North Atlantic
and Arctic Oceans)

Werewolf
(North America
& Europe)

Mermaid
(worldwide)

Most mythical creatures are the stuff of nightmares. So why do we like them? Because they are exciting and have amazing adventures? Because they inspire us to create our own games and fantasies? Or because their stories help us to cope with real-life scary feelings?

Where else to meet a monster? Cyberspace!

Films, TV, and computer games all feature fearsome mythical creatures. Something strange—and scary—may be flickering right now on a screen near you!

Vampire
(Eastern Europe)

Dragon
(China)

Cyclops
(Greece)

Medusa
(Greece)

Minotaur
(Crete)

Yeti
(Himalayas, Asia)

Ten mythical creatures are featured in this book. But there are thousands—maybe millions—of others. Worldwide, these creatures are often the same, because we all share similar hopes and fears and dreams.

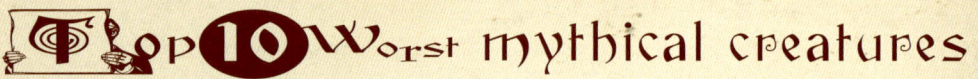

No 10
Thunderbird

Listen! Can you hear him? Thunderbird is coming! Swooping down from his home in the sky, he brings wild winds in his wings. Thunderclaps shake the world whenever he flaps his feathers. When he blinks, lightning flashes from his eyes. Don't anger him, or he'll send floods and storms to destroy you!

Woosh!

Whoosh

Vital statistics

Name: Thunderbird
Appearance: Multicolored eagle
Size: Wingspan as wide as two canoes
Armed with: Beak, horns, talons
Home: North America
Powers: Brings violent storms

You wouldn't want to know this:

Thunderbird carries deadly snakes—like forked lightning—under his wings.

Today's weather forecast is mild, with showers of DEATH and DESTRUCTION!

Crackle!

Be prepared!
Always expect the very worst

Thunderbird vs whale

Once, a monster whale devoured all the fish in the sea. Everyone was starving! Thunderbird attacked the whale, and they fought a terrible battle. Thunderbird won, and hurled the whale deep down into the ocean, where it still lives. Or else, some say, he carried it up to his lair and ate it!

Sign of strength

With its mighty wings spread wide, a carved Thunderbird keeps watch at the top of a tall totem pole in Canada. He's a sign of strength, an honored ancestor, and a guardian.

Thunderbird lives among the clouds, at the top of a holy mountain.

Revenge of the Roc

Look out! Here it comes: the Roc, another giant bird, from Asia. It carries its lunch—an elephant!—and is ready to sink ships by dropping huge boulders onto them!

Squawk!

Help! Put me down!

11

No 9

Mermaid

Pretty but deadly, mermaids kill by mistake. They sit smiling sweetly on jagged rocks, beckoning sailors to jump from passing ships to join them. Or they clasp sailors in their loving arms and take them to mermaid palaces underwater. Either way, the sailors drown, of course…

Vital Statistics

Name: Mermaid
Appearance: Half woman, half fish
Size: Up to 200 feet— about 60 meters— long.
Armed with: Sweet voice, long hair (sometimes green!), pretty face, bare bosom
Home: Rocky shores
Powers: Fatal charm

You wouldn't want to know this:

Seeing a mermaid always brings dreadful disaster.

There are mermen, too, but they don't wreck ships or kill sailors.

Hello, sailor!

Be prepared!
Always expect the very worst

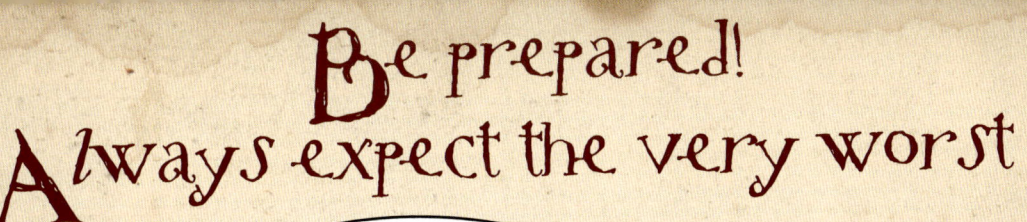

"You seem to have made a mer~stake!"

Mistaken identity

This gentle sea creature has an appealing face and a friendly, inquisitive nature. But no, it's not a mermaid, as past sailors thought. It's a real-life sea cow, or manatee!

Spirit of the waters

You may see Mami Wata gliding through West African waves, or admiring her face in a mirror. But whenever you meet her, beware! Her brilliant jewelry can blind you!

Sinister singers

Sirens are monstrous sisters (half bird, half girl) who made the best music in the world. But hearing their songs lured sailors on to dangerous rocks—and then the Sirens devoured them!

Tra~la~la!

Sparkle!

The Sirens sang in ancient Greece over 2,000 years ago.

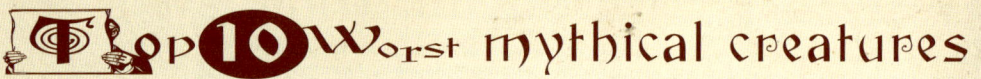

No 8

Cyclops

He's got a big, strong body, but a small and silly brain. Like most other mythical giants, the Cyclops was stupid. He trapped Greek hero Odysseus in a cave—ready to eat him— but Odysseus tricked him, blinded him, and escaped. The Cyclops' size and strength were no match for human intelligence.

Roar!

Vital Statistics

Name: Cyclops
Appearance: Lumbering, one-eyed giant
Size: Enormous!
Armed with: Massive club, spear
Home: Ancient Greece
Powers: Brute strengh

You wouldn't want to know this:

The Cyclops was a cannibal. He scooped up men and ate them, alive!

Har har!

The giant Goliath was nearly 10 feet (3 m) tall. The story of David and Goliath appears in the Bible.

Be prepared!
Always expect the very worst

I think I'll buy myself a big, sharp axe . . .

Gleam!

Sniff, sniff, sniff!

In the fairy tale, young Jack climbed a tall beanstalk to reach a giant's castle. But the giant was greedy, ravenously hungry, and had a very keen sense of smell! How did Jack escape? The giant's wife took pity on him, and helped him.

Record breaker

There are giants in the real world, as well as in myths and fairy tales. Sultan Kösen (born 1982), a farmer from Turkey, holds the world record as today's tallest man.

Sultan Kösen (on the right) is 8.1 feet (2.47 m) tall.

Giant killer

For 40 days, the giant warrior Goliath challenged the Israelites. But no one dared fight him— except for young David. He killed Goliath with just one pebble, hurled from a sling.

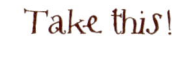

Take this!

15

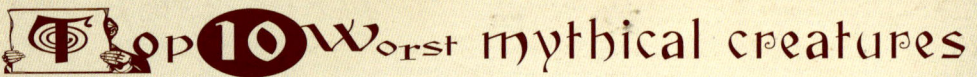

No 9

Kraken

Deep in the ocean lurks a mighty monster: Kraken. Big as an island! Looks like a giant squid! Its huge, bulging body makes fearsome whirlpools as it swims along, and its waving tentacles can pull the largest ships to the bottom of the sea.

Help! The kraken's crackin' the ship!

Vital statistics

Name:	Kraken
Appearance:	Like a giant squid
Size:	Sixty-five feet (20 m) or more
Armed with:	Tentacles, sharp beak
Home:	Atlantic and Arctic Oceans
Powers:	Wrecks ships; drowns sailors

You wouldn't want to know this:

Kraken eats small fish and belches them up, before eating the bigger fish that come to feast on the chewed-up fish. Yuck!

Splash!

16

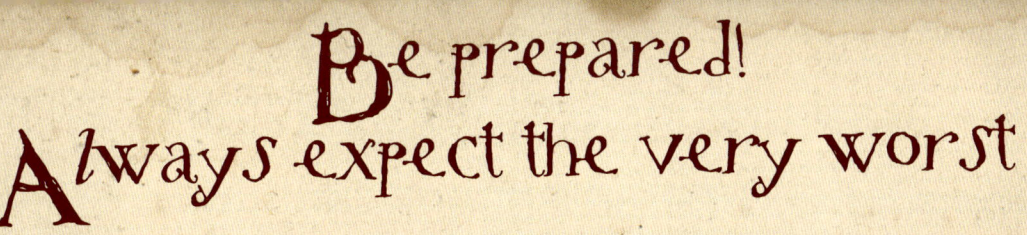

Be prepared!
Always expect the very worst

Colossal Squid

A real-life monster, the colossal squid is 46 feet (14 m) long. It has tentacles covered with sharp hooks and the largest eyes of any living creature.

Colossal squid

Gargle!

Blue whale

Giant eye

Tentacles

Predator X

Chomp!

What is the deadliest creature ever to swim in the sea? "Predator X," a fossil pliosaur (prehistoric reptile) discovered in 2008. It is 147 million years old. It was an immense 49 feet (15 m) long and had incredibly strong jaws and horribly sharp teeth.

Sure, I'm big, but that doesn't make me bad!

Mega-monster

He makes the sea boil! He leaps up to eat the sun! And, according to Bible stories, the proud and fearless Leviathan is the biggest creature on Earth.

17

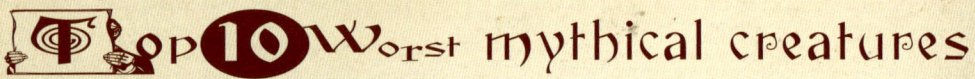

No 6

The Minotaur

The Minotaur had the mind of a man, but the head and horns of a bull. He was tragic and terrible, fierce and furious, neither man nor beast, but a mixture of both. His mother's husband, King Minos of Crete, had a special maze built to hide him, called the Labyrinth.

Snort!

Bull's head and horns

You won't like me when I'm angry... or annoyed... or mildly peeved!

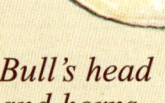 ### Vital statistics

Name: Minotaur
Appearance: Part human, part bull
Size: Like a mighty man
Armed with: Superhuman strength
Home: Crete, a Greek island
Powers: Preyed on human flesh

You wouldn't want to know this:

Seven girls and seven boys were fed to the Minotaur every year.

18

Man's body

Be prepared!
Always expect the very worst

Wrestle!

Killer hero

Theseus was not only the son of a Greek god, but also a prince, athlete, and dancer. He entered the Labyrinth, trailing thread behind him. He killed the Minotaur, then followed the thread out again. He was the only man ever to leave the Labyrinth alive.

Painting of bull dancers from King Minos' palace (c. 1500 B.C.).

Fearsome face, foul heart

Like the Minotaur, the Manticore was a hybrid (a mixture of more than one animal). It had a human head, a lion's body, and a poisonous scorpion's tail. It was truly deadly.

Grrr!

The Manticore was a symbol of the bad side of human nature.

The dance of death

Seize a fierce bull by the horns, then somersault over its back. You landed safely? You're lucky! Gored to death? You're a human sacrifice to the Greek gods!

19

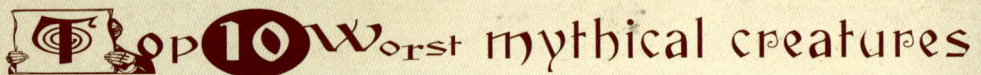

No 5

The Yeti

"Almost human"... what an insult!

A joke, a mystery, a hoax, a prehistoric human, or an undiscovered species of ape? For over 100 years, people have been puzzled about the Yeti. Some say it is a real creature that leaves tracks on snowy mountains. Others say that it simply does not exist!

Flat face, almost human

Huge, bearlike chest

Long, strong arms

Thick, shaggy hair

Giant feet

Vital statistics

Name: Yeti

Appearance: Very hairy, huge feet, sharp claws

Size: Up to 10 feet (3 m) tall

Armed with: Stealth and strength

Home: Himalaya region in Tibet, China, India

Powers: Rides horses and yaks; survives in snowy wilderness

You wouldn't want to know this:

Some reports say that Yetis kidnap humans and keep them as pets.

Be prepared!
Always expect the very worst

Early explorers

Since 1832, European explorers in the Himalayan mountain range of Asia have reported sightings of a strange wild creature that left mysterious tracks in the snow.

Bigfoot

What leaves footprints over 2 feet (61 cm) long and 7.9 inches (20 cm) wide? "Bigfoot," a monster like the Yeti that is said to live in the Pacific Northwest of North America.

Several people claimed to have seen Bigfoot. Film footage showing a huge, hairy creature, almost 10 feet (3 m) tall, was recorded in California in 1967. But who knows whether the pictures were fake or real?

lurk!

Under the microscope

Imagine the excitement when explorers found clumps of "Yeti" hair in a Tibetan monastery! But in 2008, scientists proved that the hair came from a goral. A goral is a Himalayan animal a bit like a goat. What a disappointment!

21

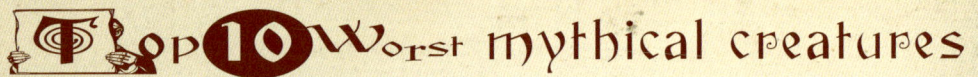

 № 4

Werewolf

What would it be like to change shape, to be transformed into an animal? That's what happens to werewolves, mostly during a full moon. One minute, they're a normal person, the next, they have hairy skin, huge fangs, drooling jaws—and a hunger for dead bodies!

Vital statistics

Name:	Werewolf
Appearance:	Wolf standing upright like a human
Size:	Large, lean, hungry wolf
Armed with:	Sharp fangs and strong jaws
Home:	Europe, North America
Powers:	Kills; eats corpses; steals children

You wouldn't want to know this:

Women werewolves have poisonous claws—and can kill children just by looking at them!

Howwwl! Grrrrr! Snarrrl!

It is said that a werewolf can only be killed by a silver bullet.

Be prepared!
Always expect the very worst

Spot a werewolf: handy checklist

- Curved fingernails
- Ears low on head
- Eyebrows meet over the nose
- Bristles under the tongue

Hmm, should I see a doctor or eat one?

How to become a werewolf

- Be bitten by a werewolf
- Rub body with magic ointment
- Drink special potion
- Be cursed by holy person
- Drink water from werewolf's footprint
- Put on wolfskin belt
- Sleep outside, under a full moon

I always seem to get hungry during a full moon!

Monster baby?

Strange creatures with snarling faces and wolflike fangs appear in myths from many different lands. Most famous are "were-jaguars"—half human, half jaguar— from the Olmec civilization of Central America.

Split head

Snarling mouth

Hands like paws

Olmec stone carving of were-jaguar made around 1000 B.C.

Wolf warriors

In Viking times (around A.D. 800–1100) fighting men joined elite teams of wolf-warriors, the Ulfhednar. They dressed in wolfskins, making them look like werewolves, and worked themselves into a savage killing frenzy before battle.

Arooooo!

23

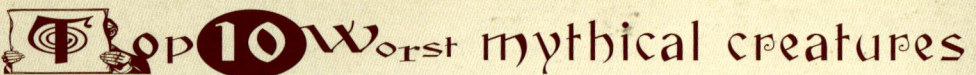

 No 3

Medusa the Gorgon

Medusa was born beautiful, with wonderful, wavy hair. But she dared to say that she looked as good as the goddess Athena. Outraged, Athena turned Medusa's hair into snakes, her teeth into tusks, and her hands into cold metal. Athena's final curse? Making Medusa's eyes turn men to stone. No one would look at her now!

Hiss!

Spit!

Look at me when I'm talking to you!

Vital statistics

Name: Gorgon
Appearance: Very ugly: staring eyes, snakes for hair, ghastly grin
Size: Tall woman
Armed with: Snakes, tusks, bronze hands, golden wings
Home: Ancient Greece
Powers: Deadly gaze

You wouldn't want to know this:

Just one drop of Medusa's blood could kill. It was also used as powerful —but dangerous—medicine.

Be prepared!
Always expect the very worst

Aha! Gotcha!

Mirror, Mirror

How can you kill a Gorgon without being turned to stone? Greek hero Perseus used his shield as a mirror so his eyes wouldn't meet Medusa's gaze, and he cut off her head!

Awful Warning

The Greek goddess Athena wore Medusa's head on the front of her armor. It sent out an awful warning: "I'm mighty and dangerous! Keep away!" Gorgon heads were carved on Greek temples, too, to stop evil spirits from entering.

What's in a name?

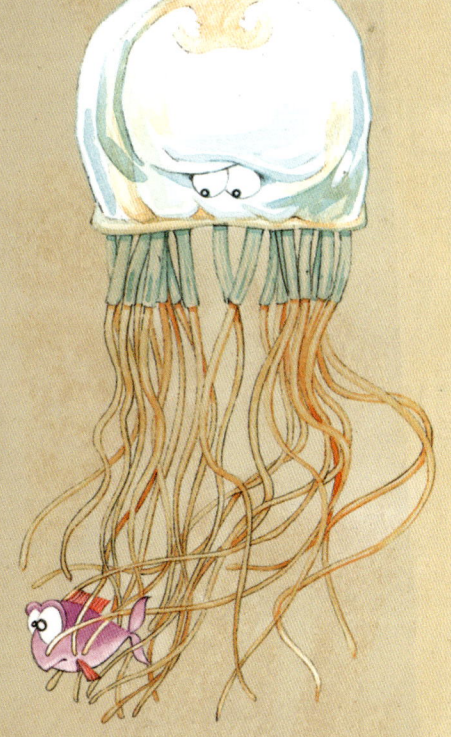

Some kinds of jellyfish have the name "Medusa" because their long, trailing tentacles look like her snaky hair.

Don't look now!

Like Medusa, the Basilisk killed with a single glance. A very strange creature, it was hatched by a rooster from a serpent's egg, spat fire, and trailed poisonous slime.

Cluck!

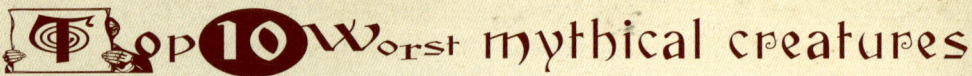

 No 2

Vampire

Dead but undead! Vampires cannot rest in peace, but haunt the world of the living, longing for fresh blood. Greed and violence are their only pleasures; they do not care how many they devour. Loathed and feared, they are outcasts forever—unless they are caught and killed (again!) in horrid and revolting ways.

Sinister cloak, like a bat's wings

Mwahahaha!

Come closer! Very close! There's nothing to fear...

Vital statistics

Name: Vampire

Appearance: Deathly pale (or dark red), burning eyes, hairy palms

Size: From thin and hungry to bloated and swollen

Armed with: Fangs, claws, sinister smile

Home: Primarily Eastern Europe, but also worldwide

Powers: Bloodsucker!

You wouldn't want to know this:

Just one bite from a vampire will make you a vampire, too.

Be prepared!
Always expect the very worst

Evil Omen

Roman myths told how the Strix (screech owl) was once a woman, but she ate human flesh and blood, and became a vampire bird.

Seeing the Strix brought bad luck.

screeeeech!

Vampire-proof?

Vampires hate garlic and can't cross running water. The best advice? Don't let them near enough to kiss or bite you!

Worldwide Horror

Vampire myths come from many lands. In Mexico, the Aztec Cihuateotl (Night Demon) stole children, sent madness, and drank blood.

I may be small, but I sure make you suffer!

Mighty Bite!

Vampires are not the only creatures to suck blood. Tiny insects, such as mosquitoes and bedbugs, also feast on it. Their bites itch, bleed, and spread dangerous diseases. Ugh!

Itch!

27

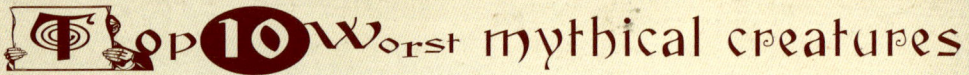

No 1

Dragon

Marvel or monster? The dragon is both. Its size, strength, and wisdom give it great powers to help or do harm. In Chinese myths, dragons mostly guard and guide—though they are awesomely awful when angry. Elsewhere in the world, dragons mean danger. They snatch and swallow victims, and their fiery breath destroys whole kingdoms. They also smell foul!

Chinese dragon

Roar!

Vital statistics

Name: Dragon (Chinese)
Appearance: Snake with legs
Size: Small as a silkworm, big as the world
Armed with: Sharp teeth and claws
Home: Up among rainclouds in the sky
Powers: Control the weather; guard emperors; become invisible; glow in the dark

You wouldn't want to know this:

Angry dragons send disastrous tsunamis and floods.

Be prepared!
Always expect the very worst

Devil in disguise

Outside China, dragons are fierce, cruel devils. They delight in evil, and kill to win hoards of golden treasure.

It's mine! All mine!

Many-headed monster

Greek myths tell how the hero Heracles fought the Hydra, a many-headed dragon. As he sliced heads off with his sword, more grew to replace them.

Hisss!

Spit!

Dragon of doom

Jörmungandr, the World Serpent, appears in myths from Viking lands. He wraps himself around the world, holding his tail in his mouth. When he lets go, the world will end!

Grrrr!

England's hero?

George, the patron saint of England, is famous for killing a dragon. But his story is a myth, in praise of courage. George probably never lived— but neither did dragons!

Stab!

Glossary

Ancestor A blood relative who lived many, many years ago.

Ancient Referring to something that existed before the 5th century A.D.

Athena The ancient Greek goddess of wisdom and strength.

Bronze A metal made of copper and tin.

Corpse The dead body of a person or animal.

Cyberspace Another word for the immense collection of Web sites brought together by the Internet.

Emperor The leader of an empire.

Fangs Long, pointed teeth often found in meat-eating animals and also in fantasy creatures like vampires and dragons.

Goral A goatlike animal found in different parts of Asia.

Guardian Someone or something that looks after, or guards, a precious item, person, or animal.

Himalayas A vast mountain range which stretches across several countries in Asia.

Hoax A trick played on the general public to make them believe something that isn't true.

Hybrid A combination of two or more different things.

Hydra The many-headed water beast that was killed by the ancient Greek hero Heracles.

Inquisitive Likes to ask a lot of questions.

Israelites In the Bible, the descendants of Jacob.

Jaguar A big cat found in North and South America.

Labyrinth In ancient Greek mythology, the maze that was built to hold the Minotaur.

Manatee (or sea cow) A large friendly mammal that lives in the sea.

Monastery A building, or group of buildings, devoted to the practice of religion.

Myth A story told in ancient times, often associated with religion.

Pliosaur A type of reptile that lived under the sea in prehistoric times.

Poison A substance that is harmful if eaten, drunk, or absorbed through the skin.

Prehistoric The period of time before recorded history.

Prey A creature that is killed for food.

Sacrifice A living creature that is killed in order to please or to calm the gods.

Silkworm A very small worm that produces silk.

Sling A folded piece of cloth used to throw something by swinging it.

Talons Sharp claws.

Tentacles Long, trailing body parts of sea creatures that often have stings, suckers, or hooks.

Tsunami A huge, destructive wave of water.

Wingspan The distance between the tip of one wing to the tip of the other.

Thunderbird

31

Top 10 Worst mythical creatures